# Pretty In **Pink**:

# 𝒫raying,
# 𝒥nfluential,
# 𝒩onsense Free,
# 𝒦ingdom Women

Dr. Jacquelyn Hadnot

©copyright 2013 Dr. Jacquelyn Hadnot

Dr. Jacquelyn Hadnot
Published by: Igniting the Fire Publishing
1314 North 38th Street
Kansas City, KS 66102
www.ignitingthefire.net

No part of this publication may be reproduced, stored in a retrieval system, or transmitted, in any form or by any means, electronic, mechanical, photocopying, recording, or otherwise, without the written prior permission of the author.

Unless otherwise noted, all Scripture quotations are taken from King James Version of the Bible.

Scripture quotations marked AMP are taken from The Amplified Bible AMP. The Amplified Bible, Old Testament copyright © 1965, 1987 by the Zondervan Corporation. The Amplified New Testament, copyright © 1954, 1958, 1987 by the Lockman Foundation. Used by permission.

Scripture quotations marked NASB are taken from The New American Standard Bible AMP. Copyright © 1960, 1962, 1963, 1968, 1971, 1972, 1973, 1975, 1977 by the Zondervan Corporation. The Amplified New Testament, copyright © 1954, 1958, 1987 by the Lockman Foundation. Used by permission.

Scripture quotations marked NIV are taken from The New International Version. Copyright © 1973, 1978, 1984 by the International Bible Society. Used by permission.

Cover Design: Dr. Jacquelyn Hadnot
Copyright© 2012 by Dr. Jacquelyn Hadnot
All rights reserved.

Please note that Igniting the Fire's publishing style capitalizes certain pronouns in Scripture that refer to the Father, Son, and Holy Spirit, and may differ from some Bible publishers' styles.

# Acknowledgements

This book is dedicated to the visionary of the Pretty in Pink Women's Conference, Dr. Cynthia Davis. She had a vision to bring women together from every area of life and ministry in order to empower them to reach for excellence.

I am honored to be a part of the vision God has given her and I count it a privilege to stand before God's women and proclaim that we are **Pretty in Pink,** *praying, influential, nonsense free, Kingdom women.*

Dr. Cynthia has given her all to this gathering of women and she has pressed forward despite the obstacles that tried to hinder her. She did not sit back and allow the enemy to get the upper hand;

she stood as a Kingdom warrior and pressed in to make this gathering of eagles happen. I believe that Pretty in Pink will do several things for the women in attendance:

- Open their minds and hearts to the purpose and destiny that is before them.

- Open dialogue that will facilitate healing.

- Create a platform for women to address issues they have been facing.

- Teach what it means to be Kingdom women.

- Become the tool for impartation, illumination and revelation from the Lord.

- Create an atmosphere of sisterhood.

Finally, Pretty in Pink will become the standard by which women everywhere can birth out retreats, conferences and workshops that will move women from the mediocre to the magnificent.

Ladies, enjoy the journey of discovery as you discover what it means to be PRETTY IN PINK.

Pretty In Pink: Praying, Influential, Nonsense Free, Kingdom Women

# Introduction

I decided to write this book in honor of the Pretty in Pink Women's Conference. When Dr. Cynthia Davis asked me to participate in this move of God, I was thrilled. The thought of helping women reach their full potential ignited a fire within me. My desire is to see women around the world go higher and grow deeper. I believe Pretty in Pink has the potential to accomplish this and more.

With the dynamic women that have been selected to cover each topic revolving around the subject of PINK, every woman with a desire for greater can reach her aspirations. Pretty in Pink is a gathering of women in its NOW season.

This book is my gift to the women of Pretty in Pink.

I hope this book will reinforce the teachings that the women will receive during the conference.

Each woman in attendance will bring a special flavor to the conference and each of us will walk away forever changed. For that, I will be eternally grateful.

Even if you do not attend the conference, I believe that this book will ignite a fire in you to experience Pretty in Pink and that you will invite it to your city.

Women, it is time to get PRETTY IN PINK.

# Contents

Acknowledgements

Introduction

| | | |
|---|---|---|
| Chapter 1 | What is **PINK**? | 13 |
| Chapter 2 | Are you a *Praying* Woman? | 17 |
| Chapter 3 | Are you a Woman of *Influence*? | 21 |
| Chapter 4 | Are you *Nonsense* Free? | 27 |
| Chapter 5 | Are you a *Kingdom* Woman? | 31 |
| Chapter 6 | He Calls You Beautiful | 37 |
| Chapter 7 | Are You Ready to be Used? | 45 |
| | About Author | 53 |
| | Books by Dr. Jacquie | 57 |
| | Journal Space | 61 |

Pretty In Pink: Praying, Influential, Nonsense Free, Kingdom Women

# Pretty In **Pink**:

# Praying,

# Influential,

# Nonsense Free,

# Kingdom Women

Igniting the Fire Publishing

Pretty In Pink: Praying, Influential, Nonsense Free, Kingdom Women

*Chapter 1*
# What is **PINK**?

What is PINK? Pink is:

## *P*raying, *I*nfluential, *N*onsense Free, *K*ingdom Women

As women, we are often required to wear many hats, sometimes wearing two or three at the same time. God created us to be flexible yet firm. We are often the ones who must set or lift up the standard. Over the years, women have gotten a bad rap being labeled troublesome, messy, and jealous or other unflattering terms. I am not saying that women are not messy at times, but I do not think that is true for all women. For the most part, mature or well-grounded women refuse to deal in nonsense and drama. It takes spiritual grounding to recognize trouble, gossip, strife and the like and destroy it at the root. Maturity or grounding is not always about your chronological age, it is about age in the spiritual sense.

I have a motto that says, "I refuse to deal in nonsense." I live by it and I will not allow anyone or anything to deter me from my nonsense free stance. If it means disconnecting with some people in order to maintain this position, then that is how it will be. I will continue to love them from a distance, but it would be a serious mistake to allow trouble to enter into the camp. I call them my taters: naysayers, player haters, spectators, instigators, and agitators. Allowing the wrong people into your life will surely bring you trouble. Nonsense is always followed by trouble, headaches and heartaches.

There are key elements that are necessary to ensure that your destiny will not be hindered when messy situations and circumstances try to infiltrate your camp.

I believe that as agents of and for change, we must set the standard from a right and righteous posture that other women can model, We must reach other women with a message of encouragement and hope. We will accomplish this when we are secure and walking in a spirit of excellence.

When the need for healing arises, we must adapt a mindset of PINK if we are to walking in the healing virtues of the Lord.

Let's look at the key components that make up the acronym PINK: *P*raying, *I*nfluential, *N*onsense Free, *K*ingdom Women. Are you a *P*raying Woman?

## Chapter 2
# Pretty in PINK:
# Are you a *P*raying Woman?

Are you a Praying woman? Prayer is the key to the kingdom. Prayer connects your heart to the heart of God. Stormie Omartian says in her book, A Book of Prayer: 365 Prayers for Victorious Living, *"Life is much better when prayer is an ongoing part of it. It helps if we can take a few moments at various times throughout each of our busy days to pause for a refreshing and comforting time of communicating with our Heavenly Father."*

As Kingdom women, prayer must be our lifestyle. We must be driven by prayer and driven to prayer. It is mandatory that our lives be bathed in prayer. We must wear the mantle of prayer. Without prayer, we will find the trials and tribulations we face daily, heavy and unbearable. Prayer brings us to the throne room of God where He can hear our heart and we can hear His. Prayer is our open communication line to the Father. Prayer  allows us to go boldly before the throne of God and obtain help in our time of need. Prayer is the place where the Lord will prepare us for battle. We will receive strategies and marching orders when we go to the Lord in prayer. Prayer is the place where we can pour our hearts out to God.

Why? Because when a righteous woman cries, the

Lord will hear and deliver us out of all our troubles. As a woman of prayer, you possess one of the strongest elements in the arsenal of warfare, prayer. As warriors for the Lord, we should be heavily armed with the Ephesians 6 armor of God.

A woman of prayer will possess the following qualities:

- ❖ She will be strong in the Lord (v 10)
- ❖ She will be strong in the power of His might (v 10)
- ❖ She will put on the whole armor of God (v 11)
- ❖ She will stand (v 13-14)
- ❖ She will girt her loins with truth (v 14)
- ❖ She will put on the breastplate of righteousness (v 14)
- ❖ She will have her feet shod with the preparation of the gospel of peace (v 15)
- ❖ She will take the shield of faith (v 16)

- ❖ She will take the helmet of salvation (v 17)
- ❖ She will take the sword of the spirit (v 17)
- ❖ She will pray in the spirit (v 18)
- ❖ She will watch in prayer (v 18)

Because you are a heavily armed praying Kingdom woman, you will have the ability to:

- ❖ Stand against every enemy (v 11-14)
- ❖ Withstand all attacks (v 13)
- ❖ Quench all the fiery darts of Satan (v 16)

Because prayer is the strength of your armor, your Commander In Chief will show you the enemies that oppose you and how to overcome them. *"With all prayer and petition pray at all times in the Spirit, and with this in view, be on the alert with all perseverance and petition for all the saints"* *(Ephesians 6:18).*

## *Chapter 3*
# Pretty in PINK:
# Are you a Woman of
# **Influence**?

As a woman of influence, you are called to be an agent of and for change.

*"Deborah, a prophetess, the wife of Lappidoth, was leading Israel at that time. She held court under the Palm of Deborah between Ramah and Bethel in the hill country of Ephraim, and the Israelites came to her to have their disputes decided"* (Judges 4:4-5). Deborah was a leader in Israel and she was *a*

*woman of influence.*

*One of those listening was a woman named Lydia, a dealer in purple cloth from the city of Thyatira, who was a worshiper of God. The Lord opened her heart to respond to Paul's message. When she and the members of her household were baptized, she invited us to her home. "If you consider me a believer in the Lord," she said, "come and stay at my house" And she persuaded us* (Acts 16:14:15). Lydia persuaded Paul's team to come to her house, she was *a woman of influence.*

*"Now in Joppa there was a disciple named Tabitha (which translated in Greek is called Dorcas); this woman was abounding with deeds of kindness and charity which she continually did"* (Acts 9:36). Tabitha was kind and charitable and *a woman of influence.*

Do you possess the character and integrity necessary to be called a woman of influence? Do people look to you for answers? Do co-workers and peers look to you for direction? Can you be relied on when problems arise? Are you a servant leader?

As a woman of influence, you need the following leadership qualities:

- Character
- Charisma
- Commitment
- Compassion
- Competence
- Convictions
- Courage

God is raising up women to be about His business of Kingdom building. He is not calling us to build bigger buildings, He is calling us to build up people.

As influential Kingdom women, we must walk in the **Koach (Ko - akh)** power of God. Koach means vigor, strength force, capacity, power, wealth, means or substance. Generally, it means capacity or ability. *"But you shall [earnestly] remember the Lord your God, for it is He Who gives you power (KOACH) to get wealth,*  *that He may establish His covenant which He swore to your fathers, as it is this day"* (Deuteronomy 8:18).

The Lord has endowed you with vigor, strength force, capacity, power, wealth, means and substance in order to accomplish a great work in the earth. You may not see it in the natural, but your influence and power transcend the natural realm because your endowment comes from the spiritual realm. Therefore, the more you are in alignment with the plan of God, the more your Koach power will cause you to bear fruit.

It is vital that you operate with character and integrity in your sphere of influence because as a standard lifter, people are watching you. Remember, you are an agent of and for change for the Kingdom of God. Therefore, you are called to a higher standard. You are called to be the vessel to go in and set a standard for others to follow. As a woman of influence, you are the agent of change that Matthew 11:12 speaks of: *"And from the days of John the Baptist until now the kingdom of heaven suffereth violence, and the violent take it by force."* It is time to take it for the King and for the Kingdom.

Pretty In Pink: Praying, Influential, Nonsense Free, Kingdom Women

## *Chapter 4*
# Pretty in PINK:
# Are you *N*onsense Free?

I live by a simple motto: *"I don't deal in nonsense."* One of the fastest ways to draw fire from the enemy is to allow drama, distractions, confusion, disorder or **NONSENSE** into your life. You will become focused on the different plans, schemes and traps used to deceive, enslave or entrap you and it will cause you to loose focus on the things of God.

As a Kingdom woman, it is vital that you are connected to the vine in every area of your life.

This will ensure that you are prepared when the enemy tries to insinuate NONSENSE into your life. The enemy will step to you with tricks, traps and snares that have one purpose, to knock you off your post.

Have you ever had someone call you with a problem, dump on you and leave you feeling drained and strained? When this happens, you will be left feeling weighed down with the problems of others. The moment you are weighed down with a spirit of heaviness, that is the moment the enemy strikes with stealth precision.

Helping others is part of our assignment, but being drawn into a trick, trap or snare IS NOT. You must realize when the enemy is planting a trap to ensnare you. Prayer is the key to recognizing the wiles of the enemy. Prayer will open your spiritual discernment to the wiles of the enemy.

Know your strengths and weaknesses and work on them both. Do not leave open doors or gateways for the enemy to have access.

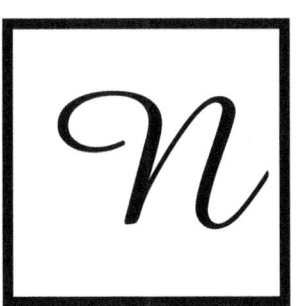

There are awesome things in store for you, your requirement is to walk it out. Walk through the doors that God opens for you and do not look back at the doors He closes. Stand firm in your place in God and know without a doubt that you are a woman of purpose and destiny.[1]

As much as possible strive to live a NONSENSE free life.

*If it be possible, as much as lieth in you, live peaceably with all men* (Romans 12:18).

*For kings, and for all that are in authority; that we may lead a quiet and peaceable life in all godliness and honesty* (1Timothy 2:2).

## Chapter 5
# Pretty in PINK: Are you a *Kingdom* Woman?

Are you a Kingdom woman? Do you know what it takes to be a Kingdom woman? If you are not a Kingdom woman, do you know what is keeping you from being a Kingdom woman?

I have compiled a list of seven essentials and twenty-eight characteristics of a Kingdom woman. The complete list is in my book, *"A Woman of Worth: Dressed to Heal."* I pray that it will help you on your journey of becoming a Kingdom woman.

## Essentials of a Kingdom Woman

There are seven essentials of a Kingdom woman.

- ❖ Submission
- ❖ Passion
- ❖ Character and Integrity
- ❖ Discipline
- ❖ Vision
- ❖ Power or Strength
- ❖ Excellence

Do you walk in the essentials necessary to be a Kingdom woman? If not, let's work on it, we are all works in process.

## Characteristics of a Kingdom Woman

There are twenty-eight characteristics of a Kingdom woman based on Psalm 37.

1. She controls her feelings (v. 1, 7, and 8).

2. She is free from jealousy and envy (v.1).
3. She has absolute trust in God (v. 3, 5, & 40).
4. She is set apart to do good (v. 3).
5. She constantly delights in God (v. 4).
6. She maintains a life dedicated to God (v. 5).
7. She holds onto unwavering faith (v. 5).
8. She has total dependence on God (v. 7, 9, 39).
9. She is free from anger and wrath (v. 8).
10. She walks in humility (v. 11).
11. She has an abundance of peace (v. 11).
12. She is content with her place in life (vv 16-19).
13. She is unashamed in evil times (v. 19).
14. She is compassionate and giving (vv. 21-24).
15. She is obedient to God's directions (v. 23).
16. In hardships, the Lord is there for her (v. 24).
17. Her household is blessed (v. 26).
18. She walks in righteousness (vv. 21, 29, 30).
19. She possesses wisdom and justice (v. 30).

20. God's law is in her heart (vv. 31, 34).
21. She speaks truth and justice (v. 30).
22. She walks perfect and upright (v. 37).
23. She is a woman of peace & prosperity (v 37).
24. She has the salvation of the Lord (vv. 39-40).
25. She stands firm in times of trouble (v. 39).
26. The Lord is her strength in trouble (v. 39).
27. The Lord is her help and deliverer (v. 40).
28. Her refuge is in the Lord (v. 40).

A Kingdom woman is a role model for other women. She possesses strength and qualities that bring glory to God. She is able to stand and withstand with dignity and honor.

A Kingdom woman lives and breathes the Kingdom agenda. She is a consuming fire for the Lord and she will not compromise her stand for the Kingdom agenda. A Kingdom woman is also a Proverbs 31 woman with a mindset to walk in a spirit of excellence in every area of her life. *Who can find a virtuous woman? for her price is far above rubies* (Proverbs 31:10). She is clothed in strength and honor. *"Strength and honour are her clothing; and she shall rejoice in time to come"* (Proverbs 31:25). She is a wise and kind woman. *"She openeth her mouth with wisdom; and in her tongue is the law of kindness"* (Proverbs 31:26).

She walks in excellence. *"Many daughters have done virtuously, but thou excellest them all"* (Proverbs 31:29).

It is important to know that you are a capable, intelligent, and virtuous woman. You comfort and encourage, as you strive to do good in the lives of those around you. You are girded with strength;

spiritual, mental, and physical, for your God-given tasks and your arms are strong and firm. Strength and dignity are your clothing and your position is strong and secure. You are a woman who reverently and worshipfully fears the Lord, and for that, you shall be praised!² A Kingdom woman is a beautiful woman inside and out. The Lord calls you beautiful.

*Chapter 6*
# Pretty in PINK: He Calls You Beautiful

*For you created my inmost being; you knit me together in my mother's womb. I praise you because* ***I am fearfully and wonderfully made.***

(Psalm 139:13-14 emphasis added)

Do you believe that you are *"fearfully and wonderfully"* made? Do you believe that God desires to use you for a great work on the earth? Do you believe that you are in alignment for your assignment? Do you believe that you are in a season of preparation? If this is your season, will you be able to stand and withstand the pressures that go along with it?

Kingdom women come in many shapes, forms and sizes - tall, short, thin or thick madams. We come in every race, color and creed. No two Kingdom women are alike. We are unique to the divine design of God because He fearfully and wonderfully created us.

Like a river, our layers run deep, like a river, we are constantly flowing in a deep vein called life. Moreover, like a river we can shift with the tides of life.

Our inner beauty can be as captivating as our physical beauty. Armed with the mind and heart of God, we are unmovable, unshakable, and ready to stand our ground and war in the natural and in the spiritual realm. We are mighty through God ready to pull down strongholds and cast down every imagination that exalts itself against the knowledge of God and His purpose for our lives (2 Corinthians 10: 4-5 paraphrased).

Kingdom women are strong, fragile, and fearless while at the same time watchful. We can hold our own in the boardroom and yet be submissive in the bedroom. Kingdom women are tenacious yet flexible. No matter the situation, a Kingdom woman is adaptable. Why? A Kingdom woman with her many layers and nuances is comfortable in the skin she lives in. We are created with the "spirit of excellence" of the Lord. God created us to fulfill a work on the earth. Work that requires strength, humility, passion, compassion, obedience, trust and faith - faith in God and faith in ourselves. We were not created to simply walk around bare foot and pregnant. We were not created to serve and never be served. We were created to be celebrated and not simply tolerated.[3]

As a woman of God, you are in a unique position because a plan is already prepared for you. Your assignment if you decide to accept it, is to represent the King of Kings as His ambassador.

You are also a woman after God's own heart and He has a purpose and plan for your life. Therefore, it is imperative that you stay connected to the vine. Jesus tells us in John 15:1-2, *"I am the true vine, and My Father is the vinedresser. "Every branch in Me that does not bear fruit, He takes away; and every branch that bears fruit, He prunes it so that it may bear more fruit."*

My Kingdom sister, whatever God is calling you to, He will see you through. He will give you the plan, direction and provision for the vision. Your mandate is to abide in the Lord so that you can bear fruit for the Kingdom, *"Abide in Me, and I in you. As the branch cannot bear fruit of itself unless it abides in the vine, so neither can you unless you abide in Me"* (John 15:4). *"If you abide in Me, and My words abide in you, ask whatever you wish, and it will be done for you"* (John 15:7).

You are Pretty in *P.I.N.K.* You are a PRAYING, INFLUENTIAL, NONSENSE FREE, KINGDOM WOMAN with a mandate from the King to accomplish great things for the Kingdom. The kingdom of heaven suffers violence, and PRAYING, INFLUENTIAL, NONSENSE FREE, KINGDOM WOMEN take it by force.

Arise, woman of God to the purpose and plan that God has for you. *"For I know the plans I have for you," declares the LORD, "plans to prosper you and not to harm you, plans to give you hope and a future"* (Jeremiah 29:11).

With God, all things in your life are possible. Never doubt His mighty hand when trials come because *the trial of your faith, being much more precious than of gold that perisheth, though it be tried with fire, might be found unto praise and honour and glory at the appearing of Jesus Christ* (1Peter 1:7). The trial of your faith is precious to God when you are able to stand and withstand. Know that your season of preparation will have trials. The trials are there to strengthen you for your journey. Therefore, walk it out and give the glory to God.

As you walk into your destiny, know that the Lord has your back and He is upholding you with His right hand. He loves you and wants the best for you.

You are P.I.N.K. so never settle for less than God's best. *"No good thing does He withhold from those who walk uprightly"* (Psalm 84:11). Walk upright before the Lord and He will exalt you in due season if you do not faint. Live in His presence and arise to the destiny that is set before you. Are You Ready to Be Used?

Pretty In Pink: Praying, Influential, Nonsense Free, Kingdom Women

## *Chapter 7*
# Pretty in PINK:
# Are You Ready to Be Used?

What elements are needed to ensure that you are a vessel ready for the master's use?

1. Are you **diligent**?
2. Are you **obedient**?
3. Do you walk in **integrity**?
4. Do you possess a **solid character**?
5. Are you a **virtuous woman**?
6. Can you **stand and withstand** in warfare?
7. Are you in tune with the **times and seasons** in your life?

*"Therefore, if anyone cleanses himself from these things, he will be a vessel for honor, sanctified, useful to the Master, prepared for every good work"* (2 Timothy 2:21).

Use the journal space at the end of this book to answer the seven questions above. Your answers will help you face the issues that can keep you from being ready to be used by God. Your ability to look in the mirror and be honest will go a long way in being ready when your time of revealing arrives.

Take a spiritual inventory of your place in God. Pray Psalm 139 and allow the Lord to lead you in the direction He desires. *"Search me, O God, and know my heart; test me and know my anxious thoughts. See if there is any offensive way in me"* (Psalm 139:23-24). Do your ways offend God? If so, it is time to pull the covers back and allow the

Lord to expose the offensive ways and cleanse you of all unrighteousness. The worst thing you can do is cover up that which offends God and eventually wind up having it exposed as you go forth in your assignment. You will hit a brick wall and never receive the fullness of God. You will have a modicum of success, but it will never be at the level or dimension God desires for you.

Have you been cleansed from the hurts and pains of your past? Are you a vessel that the Lord can fill with His anointing? Will you be able to walk into the full plan for your life with excess baggage on your shoulders? Will the stains and pains of your past taint the oil in your box?

The oil that you carry is priceless, and it is precious, do not take it lightly. The best place for you is on your face, in God's face, that is the safest place you will ever find. Protect the oil, guard your anointing and stay the course because God has a great destiny for you. You must protect the oil of the Lord because the oil you carry will bring healing to the nations. When I say nations, I am speaking beyond going to other countries. The nations I speak of are right in your own back yard. Where are the nations?

- Your family - that's a nation!
- Your neighborhood - that's a nation!
- Your church - that's a nation!
- Your job - that's a nation!
- Your school - that's a nation!
- The homeless - that's a nation!
- Women on the streets - that's a nation!
- Women in prison - that's a nation!
- Women suffering under abuse, that's a nation.
- The elderly - that's a nation, too!

Many nations are waiting for the oil that you carry, so don't put God in a box. You may never leave this country, but you could bring hope and healing to hundreds, thousands, even millions right in your own sphere of influence. Allow Him to flow through every area of your life with the oil that is destined for the nations.

There is much work to be done and it is time that we come together and be about our Father's business. Our work is not about a platform, a speaking engagement, media exposure or having your name in lights. This is a work for the Kingdom that requires wisdom, courage, strength, and the power of God. You may never receive national or international recognition, but you will receive recognition for the ONE that called you for His purpose, Christ Jesus. That's all that really matters. When the Lord is pleased with you, your reward will be great.

You are not alone, you have co-laborers that are ready, willing and able to stand with you and bring the nations into the Kingdom of God. There are sisters who are ready to stand on the front line with you and hold up your arms when you are tired. Isn't it time that you reached out and grabbed another sisters arm to help hold it up? It is time that we come together as P.I.N.K. sisters and bring glory to the King. We are more than the sum of our parts. Individually we won't accomplish much, but collectively, we can accomplish great things for the Kingdom of God. Remember, the Kingdom of heaven suffers violence and violent, striving **PRAYING, INFLUENTIAL, NONSENSE FREE, KINGDOM WOMEN** take it by force.

Stay thirsty for God, remain humble before God and

the people, and stay on your face seeking God and He will exalt you in your due season.

I pray that this book has been a blessing to you. Remember, you are a Kingdom woman with a Kingdom agenda for the season of the King. Be blessed and walk into your season.

# Remember: you are B.A.D.

## Beautiful

## Amazing &

## Destined

*To accomplish great things*

# About the Author

God has called Jacquie Hadnot to encourage, inspire, motivate and activate the gifts of the Spirit in order to raise powerful ministries in the body of Christ. She is becoming a voice on the subject of prayer, worship and spiritual warfare.

She is recognized as a modern-day apostle with a strong prophetic and psalmist anointing. She has a revelational teaching ministry with a mandate to saturate the world with the Word of God. Jacquie's heart is to see people arise and walk in the destiny and inheritance of the Lord.

She founded and established It Is Written Ministries, a publication company, an accounting and consulting firm, and a global radio station. As a retired accountant and financial executive, Jacquie blends ministerial and entrepreneurial applications in her ministry to enrich and empower a diverse audience with skills and abilities to take kingdoms for the Lord Jesus Christ. A lecturer, conference speaker, teacher, business trainer, and financial consultant, she provides consulting services to businesses, churches, and individuals. She has written over twenty-five books, manuals, and other materials on intimacy with God, prayer, fasting and spiritual warfare. She has also released several music Cds and received numerous music and book publishing awards.

Beyond the pulpit, Jacquie is a talk-show host on both television and radio with her own program, Light for Your Path. Weekly she applies God's wisdom to today's world solutions. Her ministry goal is to make Christ's teachings relevant for today. She also publishes a quarterly magazine by the same name.

## About the Author

In addition to her vast experience, Jacquie has a Th.d. in Pastoral Theology and a Masters in Ministry Leadership. She is also a wife, mother of one daughter and grandmother of one grandson. She and her husband, Gregory presently pastor It Is Written Ministries in Kansas City Kansas. They also serve as owners and officers of Igniting the Fire Media Group.

Pretty In Pink: Praying, Influential, Nonsense Free, Kingdom Women

# Other Books & Materials by Dr. Jacquie

## Books in Print
- The Art of Spiritual Warfare: Strategies for Effective Warfare
- There's A Famine in the Land: *Overcoming Great Recession*
- Your Declaration of Dependence on God
- Closing the Doors to Satan's Attacks: *Overcoming Fear*
- Trapped in the Arms of Death: *Overcoming Grip of Suicide*
- The Extravagant Love of God: Experiencing the Prophetic Flow
- Cry Aloud, Spare Not! A Prophetic Call to Fast God Has Chosen
- Cry Aloud, Spare Not! The Companion-Study Guide
- His Mercy Endures Forever: Psalms, Prayers & Meditations
- To Make War with the Saints; Satan's Kingdom Agenda
- A Treasure in the Pleasure of Loving God
- Loving God through His Names: 365 Days of the Year
- Where Is Your God? Have We Lost Referential Fear of the Lord?

## Booklets
- When Fear Crept In
- Deeper…
- Naked, Broken and Unashamed

## Audio Books & Teachings
- More of You… (Volume 1)
- In the Face of Adversity: *Overcoming Life's Storms*

- Be Not Deceived…
- Where Is Your God?
- Recognizing Your Due Season
- Praying the Healing Scriptures
- The Enemy in Me: *Overcoming Self-Life Issues*
- Trusting God in a Season of Discouragement
- The Harlot Heart

## Music
- The Extravagant Love of God
- The Spoken Word of Love
- His Mercy Endures Forever: Praying the Psalms

## DVD
- When Your Faith is Being Tested
- What Made David Run
- Agents of Change
- Virtuous Women of Worship

## TO CONTACT DR. JACQUIE:
www.jacquiehadnot.com
www.ignitingthefire.net
*Write us:*
jacquie@jacquiehadnot.com

# A Woman of Worth:
*Loving the Skin I'm In*
**Also available**

## A Woman of Worth Study Guide
A comprehensive study guide designed to reinforce the teachings from the book and the conference.

## A Woman of Worth Journal
To help you on your journey of discovering the woman God pre-destined you to become. Journaling is a great way to keep your thoughts and meditations on paper.

**Coming Soon! A Woman of Worth Audio Books**

# A Woman of Worth:
*From Victim to Victor*

# A Woman of Worth:
*Dressed to Heal*
*Dressed to Heal Journal*

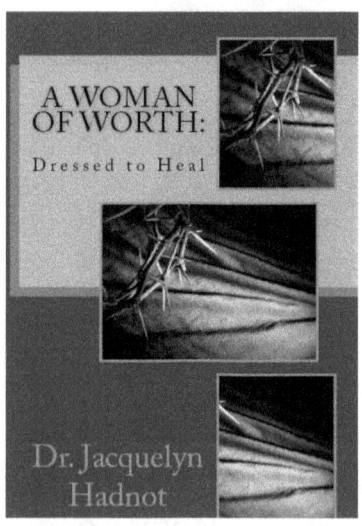

*All three in the series available*
**E-Book**

## *Journal Space*

## *Journal Space*

## *Journal Space*

## *Journal Space*

## *Journal Space*

## *Journal Space*

Pretty In Pink: Praying, Influential, Nonsense Free, Kingdom Women

## Bibliography

[1] Dr. Jacquelyn Hadnot, A Woman of Worth Loving the Skin I'm In, 2012

[2] Dr. Jacquelyn Hadnot, A Woman of Worth Loving the Skin I'm In, 2012

[3] Dr. Jacquelyn Hadnot, A Woman of Worth Loving the Skin I'm In, 2012

Pretty In Pink: Praying, Influential, Nonsense Free, Kingdom Women

Pretty In Pink: Praying, Influential, Nonsense Free, Kingdom Women